Functional Cor(
By Kristen Gos

MW01612825

The content of this book is for general instruction only. Each person's physical condition is unique. The instruction in this book is not intended to replace or interrupt the reader's relationship with a physician or other professional. Please consult your doctor for matters pertaining to your specific health.

ISBN: 978-0692094037
Title ID: 8257660

Editing: M. Peg Smith
Design & Publishing Consulting:
    The Write Place, Inc.

Table of Contents

Preface

My passion for functional sports training began to bloom in high school, following a serious knee injury. Even after physical therapy and later surgery, I wasn't the same mentally or physically. Today, with all the information I have about functional strength, I

> "Not preparing your body for sports is equivalent to riding in a car without a seatbelt."

believe I could have avoided the injury or at least have come back from it stronger than I did. My boys are now competitive athletes, and I require them to be on a science-based functional strength program or they don't compete. Not preparing your body for sports is equivalent to riding in a car without a seatbelt. Although there are no guarantees that you won't be injured, being prepared lessens the risk and can decrease the severity if there are injuries.

It's important to make informed decisions about the exercises you choose to include or exclude in your routine. Performing non-functional exercises, even performing functional exercises incorrectly, can put athletes at more risk than not exercising at all.

Safety is of predominant importance in my programs—and it's the reason I waited until now to write a book. While I want to share my knowledge and experience with the world, I also want my programs and the exercises in them implemented properly. Throughout this book you'll find photos, descriptions, and access to video demonstrations. Take time to watch and read thoroughly to ensure you have all the tools needed for success. When performed consistently and properly, the exercises in this book will make athletes more resilient to injury while improving stability, strength, and endurance on the field.

Considerations for Fully Developing the Youth Soccer Player

Play Multiple Sports

> "By about age 12, many of these specialized athletes will be passed over by kids who have fully developed their athletic minds and bodies by playing multiple sports."

While this book is meant to serve athletes whose primary sport is soccer, I recommend that young athletes play multiple sports until they reach late adolescence.

As a parent, the temptation to have a child focus solely on soccer at a young age seems logical— assuming that the more hours of soccer logged, the greater the chances for future success. It may look that way in the early years, but by about age 12, many of these specialized athletes will be passed over by kids who have fully developed their athletic minds and bodies by playing multiple sports.

In the early years, skill development is not as important as athletic development. Complementary sports that aid in developing functional core strength and athleticism for soccer include, but are not limited to, basketball, wrestling, swimming, volleyball, tennis, and lacrosse.

The trend to focus early on one sport has little to do with science. Research shows that specialized athletes are at increased risk for overuse injuries, and that early specialization in most sports actually prevents children from developing to their full potential.

In my experience, most coaches support and even encourage varied sports participation, but that's not always the case. If coaches push your child to specialize early and train year-round, have an open conversation with them about current and up-to-date research:

- A 2016 clinical report from the American Academy of Pediatrics recommends that children participate in multiple sports, at least until puberty, in order to decrease the possibility of injuries, stress, and burnout. The report also concludes that, for most sports, specializing in a sport later (late adolescence) may lead to a higher chance of young athletes accomplishing their athletic goals.

- A study published in *The Journal of Sports Sciences* compared physical fitness and gross motor coordination in boys who specialized in one sport and those who sampled more than one sport. The conclusion: At age 12, boys who played various sports were more coordinated, had more explosive strength, and were faster than those who specialized in only one.

- Dr. Matt Bowers, clinical assistant professor of kinesiology and health education at the University of Texas says, "By allowing soccer players to develop physical literacy and experience different sports—while also staying in touch with soccer—those players could see better performance at elite levels of play."

- An American Medical Society for Sports Medicine survey conducted in 2013 shows that 88 percent of college athletes surveyed participated in more than one sport as a child.

- US Youth Soccer highlights the four primary benefits of playing multiple sports: 1) mental growth, 2) physical improvements, 3) new experiences, and 4) avoiding burnout.

- The National Strength and Conditioning Association recommends that athletes play three or more sports through the age of 12, and at least two sports from ages 12 to 16 or through high school.

- A study from the School of Medicine and Public Health, University of Wisconsin, reports that high school athletes who specialize in a single sport are 70 percent more likely to suffer an injury during the playing season than athletes who play multiple sports.

Make Time for Free Play

For developing motor skills, core strength, agility, balance, and coordination, free play is essential.

Studies indicate, and some parents can verify, that the creativity of free play—without interference from adults—helps kids learn leadership skills, conflict resolution, and problem-solving.

> "For developing motor skills, core strength, agility, balance, and coordination, free play is essential."

In years past, children were more likely than they are today to organize activities within their neighborhood. Today, spontaneous (or even well-planned) games are generally replaced with adult-organized, year-round, and specialized training.

Most experts agree and studies support that less free play plus more structured training equals an overall decline in development:

- John O'Sullivan, youth soccer coach and founder of Changing the Game Project says, "Before the age of 12, unstructured free play is most important for the physical, mental, and emotional development of the youth athlete."

- A US Soccer Federation 2006 document, *Best Practices for Coaching in the United States*, advises, "Coaches can often be more helpful to a young player's development by organizing less, saying less, and allowing the players to do more. Be comfortable organizing a session that looks like pickup soccer. Young soccer players require a certain amount of uninterrupted play, which allows them to experience soccer firsthand."

- In 2007, a study published in *Physical Education and Sport Pedagogy* reports that engaging in multiple sports and free play is preferable to early involvement in practice activities and that it does not hinder sport-specific skill development. The study also reports that structured training at a young age contributes to a higher dropout rate.

- A 2013 Loyola University Medical Study shows that athletes who spend more time in unorganized free play—such as pickup games—decrease the probability for injuries while playing organized sports.

Play Fewer Organized Games

Competition encourages thinking and working at a faster pace, taking risks, following rules, managing nerves, and winning and losing with grace. However, studies show that too much competition for young athletes can negatively impact physical, mental, and emotional development.

During an organized game, players get few touches in comparison to a well-run practice or small-sided pickup game. Even for teenagers and adults, too many organized games can lead to a decline in skills, mental and physical fatigue, and injuries.

Several studies back up the theory that young athletes benefit from fewer organized games:

> **"The mean time in which an individual player is in possession of the ball during an organized match is fewer than two minutes."**

- In 2010, a study published in *The American Journal of Sports Medicine* analyzed physical performance and injury rate for athletes who played two soccer matches per week. Injury rates were shown to be significantly higher for players with two matches per week compared to one match per week.

- Tom Turner, US Youth Soccer National Instructor, says, "In the American soccer environment, it is not uncommon for aspiring young players to compete in over 100 games during the calendar year, invariably at the expense of a sound long-term individual training program."

- A 2013 Loyola University study followed 891 young athletes who were seen for sports injuries and/or sports physicals at Loyola University Medical Center and Ann & Robert H. Lurie Children's Hospital of Chicago. Injured athletes, on average, spent more than 5 times as many hours playing organized sports as they did in free play and recreation; while uninjured athletes, on average, spent only 2.6 times as many hours playing organized sports as they did in free play and recreation.

- In a study published in the *Public Library of Science,* investigative data shows the mean time in which an individual soccer player is in possession of the ball during an organized match is fewer than two minutes.

Take Time Off

Professional athletes maintain a periodized schedule for training and competition, with planned time off from their sports. Although children's growing bodies and minds also need a break, a concerning trend in youth sports is to train and compete in the same sport year-round. This trend contributes to mental and physical burnout, overuse injuries, anxiety and depression, compromised athleticism, decreased enjoyment, and increased dropout of sports altogether.

Most soccer clubs that follow the US Youth Soccer periodized schedule get it right. The problem arises when athletes participate in structured training and competition outside their clubs during off-days and off-months.

"A concerning trend in youth sports is to train and compete in the same sport year-round."

The following support the concept that young athletes benefit from brief respites from organized practice anc games:

- The *US Youth Soccer Player Development Model* states that planned time off is vitally important to avoid over-scheduling, overuse injuries, and mental burnout. Both players and coaches need time off to recharge and return to soccer reinvigorated.

- Results of a study conducted by the School of Medicine and Public Health, University of Wisconsin, show increased risk of lower-extremity injuries for athletes who participate, within the same season, on a club team and a second team.

- Certified Athletic Trainer Dave Heidloff says, "Without taking any time off from high-level activities, the body will eventually begin to wear down faster than it can repair itself. This, when kept up long enough, can result in a wide array of injuries—including tendonitis, muscle tears, and stress fractures."

Based on the previously stated research, I recommend the following for fully developing young athletes:

- **Encourage kids to sample many sports in the early years**—at least until age 11 or 12—to fully develop minds and bodies while keeping young athletes excited about sports and to minimize chances for injury.
- If, by age 12, soccer surfaces as a primary sport, young athletes might choose one or two additional sports that complement soccer.
- I recommend playing at least two sports through high school to improve overall athleticism and to avoid injury and mental burnout.
- **Before age 12, free play is more important than structured training.** Practices should include small-sided games and opportunities for creative free play without adult interference.

Dr. Mishra, founder of *Sideline Sports Doc,* offers the following recommendations for tournament play:

Take a large enough roster to give players enough rest.

Take injury complaints seriously.

Pay extra attention to pre-game nutrition and hydration.

Engage in active stretching cool-down after each game.

Ice sore areas after games to aid in recovery.

•Games like tag are a productive way to incorporate agility training into a practice without too much structure. At home and school, encourage games like hopscotch, red-light–green-light, or jump rope—along with multiple sports.

•At about age 13, while skill development begins to take precedence, free play is still of value.

•**Discourage young athletes from playing on two teams within a season, especially the same sport,** which can lead to overuse injuries and mental burnout.

•**Play no more than two matches per week with at least 72 hours between matches** to avoid increased risk of injury.

•**Limit tournaments to one per month, at most,** while considering that pre- and post-tournament practices should be light intensity.

- Depending on climate, most regions play fall soccer (August–October) and spring soccer (March–May). Most competitive programs also have training and matches during the winter. **For youth who play soccer year-round, at the very least take off a month or two after both spring and fall seasons and spend the time doing something other than soccer**—either a different organized team sport or activities such as cycling, swimming, and other fitness-related interests.
- **Every six months, take off at least two weeks from all organized sports.** Free play and pickup games are always okay—unless injuries or physical fatigue are factors. Studies show that pickup games and free play do not tax the body mentally or physically the same as structured training and competition.

To learn more about a long-term plan for developing the physical needs of youth, see National Strength and Conditioning Association (NSCA) Position Statement on Long-Term Athletic Development.
https://www.nsca.com/long-term_athletic_development_position_statement/

Parents and coaches of youth athletes:
It is imperative that you read the previous section, "Considerations for Fully Developing the Youth Soccer Player," before moving on to the "Introduction" below. If you fail to follow the guidelines in that section, the benefits of the program I prescribe in this book may not be fully realized.

Introduction

As athletes become more competitive, the method in which they train for sports becomes vitally important. The difference between a good athlete and an

> "Functional strength training is essential for injury prevention."

exceptional athlete may depend on his or her training regimen. As athletes become bigger, stronger, and more physical—while striving to stay ahead of the curve in order to compete—functional strength training becomes essential for injury prevention.

Although well-meaning athletes, parents, and coaches look to popular fitness and bodybuilding material for information on strength training, very few resources have reliable advice on sport-specific training, and most resources emphasize the bodybuilding philosophy of isolating muscle groups. Bodybuilders may have impeccable physiques. Many also have chronic injuries and few would function well on a soccer field. The bodybuilding philosophy of strength training leads to greater risks for injury on and off the field—and it negatively impacts key athletic components, such as speed, power, balance, and agility. Remember that strength is not the primary

goal of a sport-specific training program. Of major importance is functional strength— the sort of strength called for on the playing field.

Physical therapists and sports science practitioners agree that core strength is the foundation for functional movement, which will prepare athletes for sports and reduce the risk for injuries:

"The bodybuilding philosophy of strength training leads to greater risks for injury on and off the field —and it negatively impacts key athletic components, such as speed, power, balance, and agility."

•A 2012 study published in the The Journal of Strength and Conditioning Research, which tests the effect of core strength on power, finds that core strength has a significant effect on an athlete's ability to create and transfer forces.

•Susan Karpinski, health promotion coordinator and certified strength and conditioning specialist, states, "Core strength is critical to all basic movement patterns—athlete or not."

- Leanne Griesemer, physical therapy assistant at Apex Physical Therapy, asserts, "Since your core makes up the center of your body and encompasses the spinal column, all movements pass through it. Having strong core stabilizers enables you to maximize strength in your arms and legs."

- An article by Ace Physical Therapy and Sports Medicine Institute agrees: "Core strength is vital for the essential support that helps you avoid injuries while moving in a variety of activities."

Now that it's clear how integral the core is to athletic movement and support, let's explore the muscles of the core.

What is the Core?

The muscles in the region of the body that are called the core work together to support the spine and initiate power for everyday tasks as well as athletic moves. The deep muscles located in the abdominals and low back are the most important of this group. They include the transverse abdominis, the internal obliques, the multificus (small muscles that connect to the spinal column), pelvic floor muscles, and diaphragm.

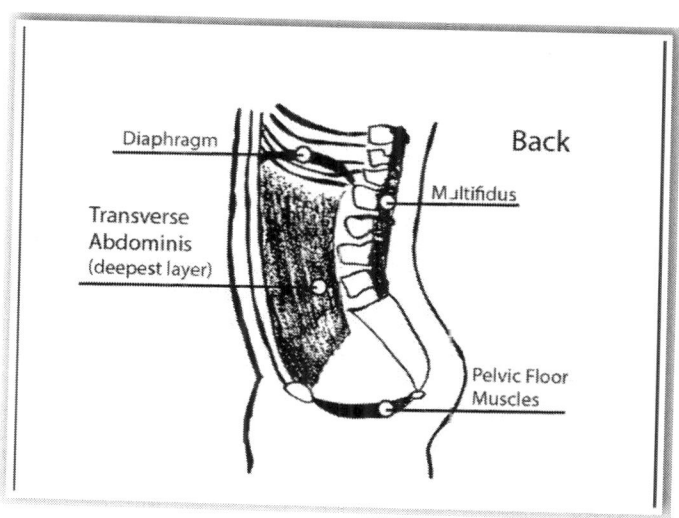

Diaphragm

Back

Transverse
Abdominis
(deepest layer)

Multifidus

Pelvic Floor
Muscles

Why is the Core So Important?

A strong core is key to both improved athletic performance and injury prevention in every sport. For soccer, which requires speed, power, and endurance—while resisting physical contact from opposing players—it's especially important. And the core, more than any other muscle group, happens to be the foundation for these components. A well-trained core also helps prevent injuries. With a strong and supportive trunk, athletes can safely rely on the power and energy transferred through it while decreasing the likelihood of low-back

> "For soccer, which requires speed, power, and endurance—while resisting physical contact from opposing players—the core is especially important."

injuries or deceleration injuries of lower extremities—such as anterior cruciate ligament (knee ACL) injuries and meniscal tears.

To avoid injury, athletes should functionally prepare their core muscles before significantly increasing loads to their bones and joints with heavy weight-lifting, plyometric, or change-of-direction drills.

Abdominal Muscles

The four main abdominal muscle groups are the rectus abdominis, the transverse abdominis, and the internal and external obliques. Together these muscles protect internal organs, regulate breathing, and provide movement and stability to the trunk.

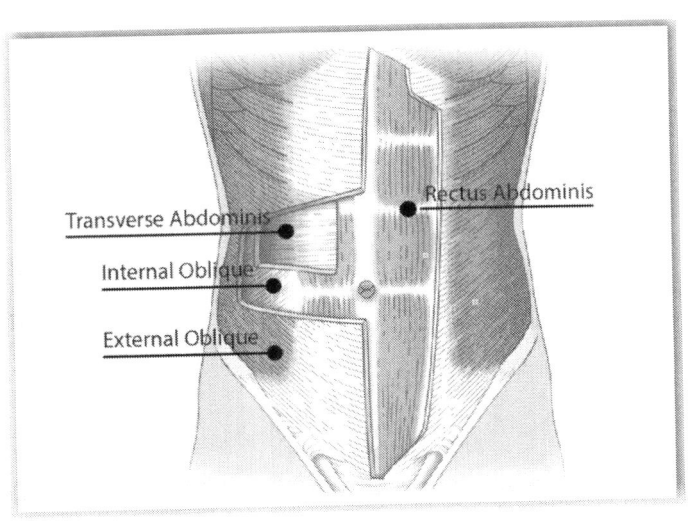

Rectus Abdominis

This muscle extends vertically on each side

> "Overdeveloping the rectus abdominis doesn't benefit athleticism and it can increase the risks of both acute and chronic back pain."

of the anterior wall of the abdomen and aids in flexing the torso forward. A highly developed rectus abdominis creates a visible "six-pack" in people who have extremely low body fat.

Overdeveloping these vanity muscles with sit-ups and crunches (see "Core Exercises to Avoid: Sit-Ups and Crunches," page 37) without focus on functional exercises that engage the deep musculature (see "Exercises for Improved Athletic Performance and Injury Prevention," pages 45–73) doesn't benefit athleticism and it can increase the risks for both acute and chronic back pain. An overtrained rectus abdominis will distend the abs and take support away from the back.

Transverse Abdominis

This most internal of all the abdominal muscles, the transverse abdominis, helps stabilize the pelvis and low back before movement. It's also where power initiates. As soccer players, this is important because when the transverse abdominis is trained properly force production is increased. In other words, athletes become more powerful shooters and faster sprinters. The transverse abdominis is also integral to creating intra-abdominal pressure and compressing the abdomen on exhalations. Both these

> "When the transverse abdominis is trained properly athletes become more powerful shooters and faster sprinters."

actions help draw in the core and bring support to the spine.

The most important action of the transverse abdominis as a soccer player is the strength and support it delivers when working to win the ball. The deep muscles in the transverse abdominis are the most active muscle group when defending physical contact. When deep core muscles are strong, players are less likely to be shoved off the ball, fall to the ground, or get injured.

Internal & External Obliques

The internal obliques lie just below the external obliques and just above the transverse abdominis. External obliques, located on the lateral sides of the abdomen, are the largest and outermost group in the mid-section.

Both muscle groups work with the rectus abdominis as well as back muscles to bend the torso to the side, and they work in synergy with each other to rotate the torso. Obliques, in conjunction with the transverse abdominis and back muscles, support the pelvis and spine; although internal obliques, the deeper of the two muscles groups, are most crucial to stabilizing the torso against extreme rotation.

Multifidus, Diaphragm, and Pelvic Floor

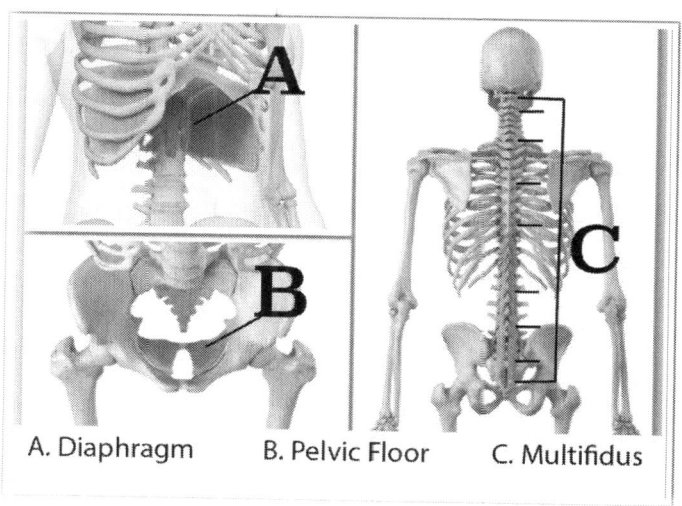

A. Diaphragm   B. Pelvic Floor   C. Multifidus

Multifidus

Key to back stability, the multifidus is a series of deep muscles that attach to the spinal column. This muscle group helps to take pressure off the spinal column and to keep the spine straight. It also aids in bending backward, sideways, and in turning and twisting. Much like the transverse abdominis, the multifidus group

> "Because soccer players make quick and powerful movements, having a strong multifidus is a major benefit."

activates in anticipation of action to protect the spine and prepare the body for movement. Because soccer players make quick and powerful movements, having this muscle strong and engaged is a major benefit.

Diaphragm

The diaphragm is a large dome-shape sheet of muscle located just below the thoracic cavity (containing the heart and lungs) and just above the abdominal cavity. It is the primary muscle needed for inhaling and exhaling, by pulling and pushing against the lungs to contract and expand.

The diaphragm also works with other core muscles to assist in stabilization. Diaphragm strength and proper breathing are essential to supply oxygen and stabilize the core during the high demand for speed and endurance while playing soccer.

Pelvic Floor

These muscles span the area beneath the pelvis and support the bladder, intestines, and (in females) the uterus. They are primarily known as the muscles that help control the bladder and bowels. In addition, they work closely with inner core muscles to enable a wide range of movement and power production that's necessary in soccer. Pelvic floor muscles also support the pelvis and spinal joints.

Core-Bracing, Diaphragmatic Breathing, Posture, and Intra-Abdominal Pressure

Core-Bracing
Learning to brace the core and having the functional strength to do so properly is essential to power production and injury prevention. Proper bracing means integrating the diaphragm, pelvic floor, and deep core muscles in order to store power for movement and to protect the spine from injury. For many, this is natural; others need to consciously practice Core-Bracing for it to become instinctive. Diaphragmatic breathing, good posture, and functional core strength are prerequisites to proper Core-Bracing.

Diaphragmatic Breathing
Good breathing mechanics means using the diaphragm rather than the chest to

> "Babies naturally expand their bellies and breathe from the diaphragm, then, along the way, many people become chest-breathers."

inhale. To determine where air is taken in when you breathe, place one hand on your belly and one hand on your chest. Notice which rises most: the belly or the chest.

Babies naturally expand their bellies and breathe from the diaphragm, then, along the way, many people become chest-breathers. Chest-breathers are at risk for chronic neck, shoulder, and back pain—along with sleeping disorders, decreased strength, and fatigue.

Not breathing into the diaphragm results in less oxygen to the blood, which is not good for long-term health. As athletes, breathing properly equals more strength and endurance on the field.

Posture

Posture, breathing, and functional core strength are intimately related. Good posture supports diaphragmatic breathing and enhances core stability, which in turn improves tolerance to high-intensity exercise and reduces the risks of muscle fatigue and injury.

The human body is designed to move rather than to sit. Today, because many children and adults spend hours hunched over electronics, expansion of the rib cage has become limited and the result is shallow breathing. The more that people sit during the day, the less the body is able to maintain a strong functional core to support proper breathing mechanics.

> "The more that people sit during the day, the less the body is able to maintain a strong functional core to support proper breathing mechanics."

Intra-Abdominal Pressure

As the diaphragm contracts and pushes down into the abdominal cavity, intra-abdominal pressure is created. To help understand the process, perform the experiment on the next page.

Intra-Abdominal Pressure Experiment

Supplies:
- 2 small paper cups
- 1 small balloon
- 1 15-pound dumbbell

Experiment:
1. Place one cup upside-down on a flat surface (such as a countertop).
2. Fill the balloon with just enough air to fit inside the second cup, without spilling out. Place the balloon-filled cup firmly upside-down beside the first cup.
3. Holding the dumbbell vertically, carefully place it on the empty cup. Notice what happens to the cup. *(Mine crushed completely in fewer than 2 seconds.)*
4. Now place the same dumbbell on the cup filled with the balloon and notice what happens. *(Mine kept its shape and was completely undamaged.)*

Imagine what could happen to your body under high loads without intra-abdominal pressure to aid in bracing your core. If you discovered that you're a chest breather, be aware of how you breathe until diaphragmatic breathing becomes natural. In addition to the health problems, without proper diaphragmatic breathing, intra-abdominal pressure will not extend to the lower lumbar spine where bracing is

34

especially important. In the Exercise Section of this book, you'll find ways to practice diaphragmatic breathing along with Core-Bracing.

What is Functional Core Training?

Whether we're talking about a warm-up, strength training, conditioning, or even nutrition, the key to a good program is functionality.

func·tion·al
adjective
1. relating to the way in which something works or operates.

As a functional nutrition specialist, I recommend foods that nourish the body to help it work and operate efficiently. A functional training program does the same —by focusing on the natural alignment and movement patterns of the body in ways that contribute to the prevention of injuries and that improve athletic performance.

Core Exercises to Avoid

Because popular media promotes core exercises that primarily focus on vanity rather than function, it's important to understand why certain exercises are not functional. When considering appropriate core exercises, avoid those that lack function or that compromise natural body alignment. For safe and functional exercises, see "Exercises for Improved Athletic Performance and Injury Prevention," pages 45–73.

> "Because popular media promotes core exercises that primarily focus on vanity rather than function, it's important to understand why certain exercises are not functional."

 Avoid these common exercises, which I advise against because they lack function and could cause injuries:

Sit Ups and Crunches

*Instead, do **Iso Abs** and **Partner CoreBracing** found in "Exercises for Improved Athletic Performance and Injury Prevention,"* pages 45–73.

Now that you understand the definition of functional and its relevance to training, it's

> "Repeatedly bending the spine can damage spinal discs over time and negatively impact posture."

understandable why crunches and sit-ups are not on my go-to list of core exercises for soccer. While sit-ups are clearly the more dangerous of the two—by putting extreme stress on bones, ligaments, and tendons in the neck and back—crunches can be harmful too. Repeatedly bending the spine can damage spinal discs over time and negatively impact posture. These two exercises are not only harmful, they also lack function. Crunches and sit-ups primarily train the top layer of muscle (the rectus abdominis) and, as discussed previously, power and stability come mostly from the deeper layer of muscle (transverse abdominis) as well as internal and external obliques.

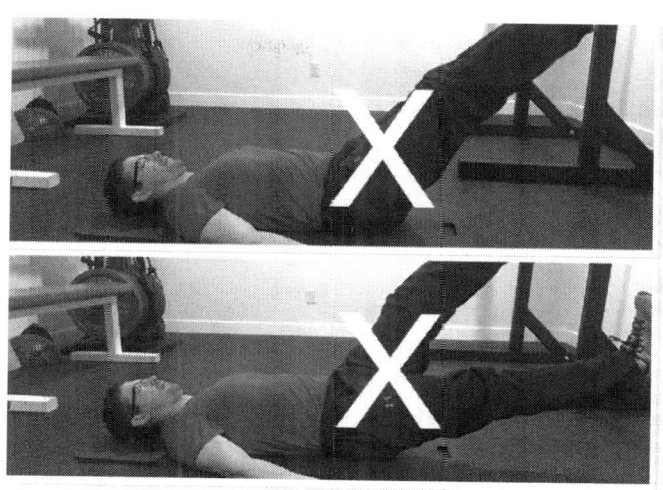

 Double-Leg-Lifts and Scissor Kicks

Instead, do **Ab Draw with Alternating Leg Up, Low-to-High Wood-Chopper,** *and* **Partner Leg Push** *found in "Exercises for Improved Athletic Performance and Injury Prevention,"* pages 45–73.

Double-leg-lifts are a sure way to make a bad back worse and injure a healthy one. A prime mover in the bottom portion of a leg lift is the psoas (hip flexor) muscle, which attaches to the vertebra in the lumbar spine. When hip flexors contract, they pull the spine into hyperextension, putting extreme pressure on spinal discs.

From a functional standpoint, consider how abs and hip flexors work together in soccer: The negative part of the movement, when

> "When hip flexors contract during a leg lift, they pull the spine into hyperextension, putting extreme pressure on spinal discs."

winding up for a shot, requires a bent leg and an isometric contraction in deep abdominals to prepare for both hip and knee extension. Sprinting, although not as pronounced, also requires intra-abdominal pressure with both hip and knee extension.

*Instead, do **Airplane** and **Bridge** found in "Exercises for Improved Athletic Performance and Injury Prevention," pages 45–73.*

Hyperextending the spine can compress lumbar discs, impinge nerves, and lead to disc herniation.

 Extreme Torso Twists - especially with weight

Instead do, **Standing Torso Rotation** *and* **Low-to-High Wood Chopper—right and left** *found in "Exercises for Improved Athletic Performance and Injury Prevention,"* pages 45–73.

The spine is not made to twist deeply, a movement which can injure disks, muscles, and tendons in the back. As a general rule, during a twist, the opposing elbow should never extend past the opposing knee.

![skull and crossbones] Leg Throw-Downs

Instead, do **Partner Core-Bracing, Ab Draw with Alternating Leg Up** *and* **Partner Leg Push** *found in "Exercises for Improved Athletic Performance and Injury Prevention,"* pages 45–73.

Leg throw-downs are an extremely dangerous core exercise. Like leg-lifts and scissor-kicks, leg throw-downs contract the psoas (hip flexor) muscle, pulling the spine into hyperextension and putting extreme pressure on spinal discs. The added resistance of having a partner forcefully throw your legs dramatically increases the pressure on discs. Even more dangerous is having legs thrown to the side. By adding a twist to an already vulnerable spine position, even the strongest of athletes are at risk for serious injury. As far as functionality of this exercise, as pointed out

"Leg throw-downs pull the spine into hyperextension and put extreme pressure on spinal discs."

earlier, athletic movements require both hip and knee extension in conjunction with Core-Bracing; leg throw-downs oppose natural movement.

Creating a Foundation

Remember: With any training program, slow and steady wins the race. Preparing the foundation is critically important. Optimally, this foundation should begin between the ages of 8 and 12, but it's never too late to start building. The exercises that follow will provide this foundation.

To prevent injuries, athletes should hold off doing heavy strength training, high-impact jumping, or high-intensity agility training until they've completed a minimum of

24 sessions each of the prescribed workouts in this book with efficiency.

(Please see "Workouts for Home or Practice Field," pages 75–78.)

Exercises For Improved Athletic Performance and Injury Prevention

Functional Standing Core Exercises

Watch my video "Dynamic Warm-Up & Core Routine Soccer" for demonstrations of these exercises at OrganicFitnessMama.com.
*Use code: **8257660***

Standing Ab Draw

Learn to do the Ab Draw properly as the first step to engaging deep abdominal muscles during exercise and sport. Pictured above is an Ab Draw holding a soccer ball, which will prepare you for the exercise that follows.

1.   While practicing good diaphragmatic breathing, from a standing position, knees bent, hips back, shoulders back, and feet a little wider than hip distance, engage your deep core (think about the muscles you'd tighten when expecting a punch to the gut).
2.   Instead of sucking in your stomach, draw the deep muscles from your belly and sides toward one another, then back toward your spine.

3. Always remember to engage your abs this way before any lifting exercise.

Standing Torso Rotation

1. From Standing Ab Draw position, hold a soccer ball in front of you, elbows in tight to the sides.
2. Rotate your torso from side to side.
3. When you are sure that the abs are properly engaged, this motion may become quicker and more powerful.

Low-to-High Wood-Chopper Center

1. From Standing Ab Draw position, hold a soccer ball in your hands— arms extended and relaxed—then push your hips back into a squat as you drop the ball between your legs (see Squat, pages 55–56).
2. With one powerful movement, arms extended, stand upright as you bring the soccer ball to the front and overhead.
3. As you perfect this exercise, add more power by accelerating up to the toes as you complete the upward movement.

Low-to-High Wood-Chopper Right

1. From Standing Ab Draw position,
    hold a soccer ball in your hands—
    arms extended and relaxed—then
    push your hips back into a squat as
    you drop the ball between your legs
    (see Squat, pages 55–56).
2. With one powerful movement, arms
    extended, stand upright as you bring
    the soccer ball diagonally to the front
    and over your right shoulder.
3. As you perfect this exercise, add
    more power by accelerating up to
    the toes as you complete the upward
    movement.

Low-to-High Wood-Chopper Left

1. From Standing Ab Draw position, hold a soccer ball in your hands— arms extended and relaxed—then push your hips back into a squat as you drop the ball between your legs (see Squat, pages 55–56).
2. With one powerful movement, arms extended, stand upright as you bring the soccer ball diagonally to the front and over your left shoulder.
3. As you perfect this exercise, add more power by accelerating up to the toes as you complete the upward movement.

Partner Core-Bracing
Right, left, top, bottom

This simple yet challenging exercise is one of the most valuable for developing a truly functional core for soccer.

1. Partner A and Partner B stand facing one another in Ab Draw position.
2. Partner A holds a soccer ball to the front, elbows in tight to sides, while Partner B adds 5 seconds of resistance to the right side of the ball, 5 seconds to the left, 5 seconds pressing down from the top, then 5 seconds pressing up from the bottom.

3. During exertion, both partners should practice Core-Bracing (see "Core-Bracing, Diaphragmatic Breathing, Posture, and Intra-Abdominal Pressure," pages 31–35), then relax the core between each phase of exertion.
4. Partners switch positions and repeat the steps.

Single-Leg Ab Draw

1. Stand on one leg, knee bent slightly to stabilize the leg; relax the raised leg.
2. While engaging the deep core, push the hips back. Imagine the muscles you'd tighten if expecting a punch to the gut. Rather than suck in the stomach, draw

the deep muscles from your belly and sides toward one another, then back toward the spine. (Always remember to engage your abs this way before any lifting exercise.)

3. Standing on the opposite leg, repeat the exercise.
4. After mastering balance with good form for at least 30 seconds, move on to Single-Leg Ab Draw with Ball Toss / Kick, below.

Single-Leg Ab Draw with Ball Toss / Kick

Younger and/or less skilled athletes should simply toss and catch the ball rather than

perform kicks. Skilled players may stand farther apart. The object is to have accurate throws and kicks that enable both partners to maintain balance throughout entire sets.

1. Partner A and Partner B, each in Single-Leg Ab Draw and each standing on the left leg, face each other about 3 to 4 feet apart.
2. Partner A tosses the ball to the right foot of Partner B, who kicks the ball to the hands of Partner A. Switch legs and repeat for a set of 10.
3. Partners change roles for tossing and kicking then repeat steps 1 and 2.

Skaters

1. From Single-Leg Ab Draw, stand on the right leg, engage the core, then Power Hop to the left leg. Work toward sticking the landing on the left leg while continuing to engage the core.
2. Hold the landing on the left leg long enough to recover balance, then hop to the right leg. Continue to stick the landing, engage the core, and balance on each hop.
3. As balance and core strength improve, push yourself to increase the distance of the hop.

Squat

Performed properly, squats are more than simple leg exercises—they are one of the best activities to learn to engage deep abdominal and back muscles for power and support of the rest of the body.

Thighs should be parallel to the floor at the bottom of the squat; however, hip and ankle mobility may limit movement for some people. If you are not able to lower to parallel while maintaining proper posture, temporarily limit the range of motion while working on flexibility.

1. From Standing Ab Draw, core engaged, sit the hips back while bending the knees and dropping the hips.
2. Shoulders should remain back, chest up, and knees in line with the ankles.
3. The back should arch slightly—without over-extending—as you descend, engaging low back muscles to support the spine.
4. Lower until thighs are parallel to the floor; then drive your weight through your heels to bring yourself back to Standing Ab Draw position.

Functional Core Exercises From the Floor

*Watch my video "End of Practice Strength and Core Routine Soccer" for demonstrations of these exercises at OrganicFitnessMama.com. Use code: **8257660***

Diaphragmatic Breathing Exercise (for chest breathers)

Initial Exercise:

1. Lie on your back, knees bent, and heels resting on a bench, chair, or sofa.
2. Place one hand on your belly and take a deep breath, expanding your belly upward. Take a few more breaths in and out. As you inhale, focus on expanding your belly both up and to the sides.
3. Try pushing a finger into each side of your belly and breathe into your fingers.
4. As you exhale, imagine bringing your ribs down.

Advanced Exercise:

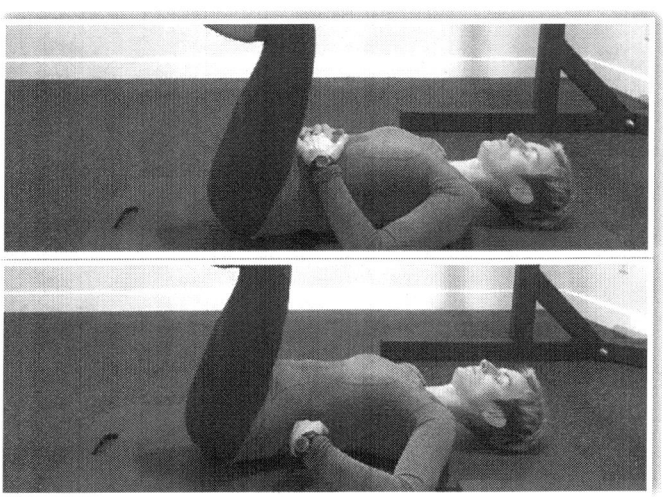

1. Try the same exercise with your legs unsupported.
2. Bend your knees at 90 degrees, directly over your hips, ankles raised.
3. To prevent your back from arching, use your deep abdominal muscles to press the small of your back against the floor.
4. Concentrate on squeezing the muscles in your pelvic floor by lifting inward as if stopping or slowing the flow of urine.
5. Place one hand on your belly and take a deep breath, expanding your belly upward. Take a few more breaths in and out. As you inhale, focus on expanding your belly both up and to the sides.
6. Try pushing a finger into each side of your belly and breathe into your fingers.
7. As you exhale, imagine bringing your ribs down.

Ab Draw

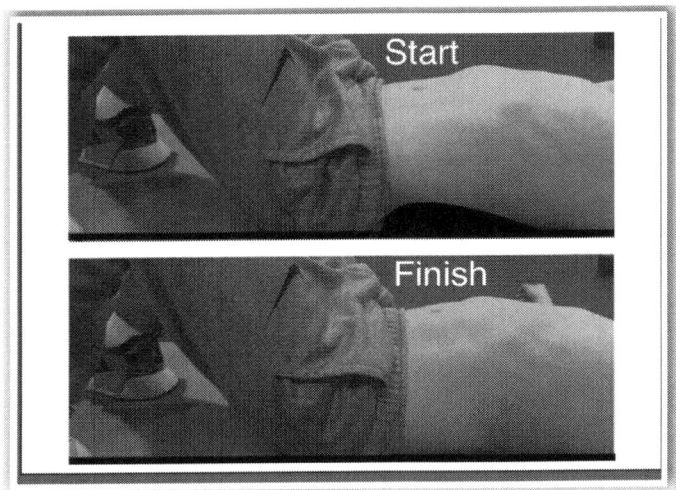

1. Lie on your back, knees bent and soles of your feet on the floor, letting your back arch naturally. You should be able to place your hands beneath the small of your back.
2. Draw your navel in toward your back while pressing your back against the floor. Be sure to use ab muscles, not leg muscles. Your hamstrings should be completely relaxed; if not, you are not engaging the ab muscles properly.
3. When you know that you are engaging your deep abs, hold the position for about 30 seconds.

Ab Draw with Alternating Leg Up

You must master Ab Draw before moving on to this exercise.

1. From Ab Draw position, abdominals engaged and back flat, lift and straighten your right leg, ankle directly over the hip (you should feel the right side of your abs become more engaged).
2. Bend your right knee as you lower your right leg, placing the sole of your foot on the floor.
3. Using the left leg, repeat steps 1 and 2, noticing the left side of your abs become more engaged.
4. Alternate sides for a court of about 20.

Partner Leg Push

You must master Ab Draw and Alternating Leg Up before moving on to this exercise. The Partner Leg Push requires enough hamstring flexibility to straighten your leg directly over your hip. If you are not properly engaging your abs and/or if your hamstrings are not appropriately flexible, the psoas (hip flexor) muscle will over-contract and pull your spine into hyperextension.

1. Partner A lies on the floor in Ab Draw position, abdominals engaged and back flat.

2. Partner B stands to the right side of Partner A in Standing Ab Draw position, feet placed near the rib cage area and in the same direction as Partner A.
3. Partner A straightens his right leg, ankle directly over the hip, then brings his left knee in toward the chest while keeping his back flat and abs engaged.
4. Partner B places his left hand on the right shin of Partner A and tries to push the straight leg toward the floor, adding enough pressure to challenge Partner A, but not so much that Partner A cannot keep his back flat and leg in position.
5. Partner A resists the pressure, keeping his leg raised and back flat.
6. Partners communicate the appropriate level of resistance.
7. Partner B moves to the left of Partner A, repeating the exercise.
8. Partners switch positions, each receiving 10 to 15 seconds of resistance on each leg.

Iso Ab
Front

1. Forearms on the floor about shoulder-width apart, elbows at a 90-degree angle and directly below the shoulders, extend your legs straight back about hip-width apart, toes on the floor.
2. Lift your body so the weight is on the forearms and toes. Your body should be in a straight line from head to heels.
3. Engage your deep core muscles by tilting the pelvis slightly and drawing in the navel toward your back (Ab Draw). Do not let your hips sag, which would disengage the abs and

put strain on the low back. (Some people suggest that the back should be completely straight, but if it takes slightly lifting your hips to properly engage your core, that's okay. It's better to lift the hips slightly than to drop the hips too low.)

Note: If you feel the need to lift your hips quite a bit to avoid back strain, modify this exercise by dropping to your knees. Be sure your back remains flat in this position so you continue to engage your abs.

Iso Ab
Side

1. From one side, place a forearm on the floor perpendicular to your body, elbow directly below your shoulder.
2. Straighten and stack your legs, then lift your hips so your weight is on your forearm and bottom foot, keeping the body in a straight line from head to heels. Place your free hand on your hip.

Note: To modify this exercise, drop to your knees and bend your legs behind you at a 90-degree angle, ensuring that your knees are in line with your hips and shoulders.

Pushup

1. Hands on the floor just wider than shoulder width, fingertips forward, arms straight (but not locked), extend your legs straight behind you with toes on the floor as you press both feet together.
2. Engage your deep core muscles by tilting your pelvis slightly and drawing your navel in toward your back (Ab Draw). Do not let your hips sag, which would disengage the abs and put strain on your low back.
3. Keep your neck in line with your spine to form a straight line from head to feet. Draw your shoulders back and down.
4. As you inhale, slowly bend your elbows, lowering your body as one unit, until your chest is about 1 inch from the floor or upper arms are parallel to the floor.
5. As you push up quickly, exhale as much air as possible.

Note: If you are not able to complete the full range of motion with perfect form, modify the pushup by dropping to your knees. Be sure your back remains flat in this position so you continue to engage your abs.

Bridge

1. Lie on your back, knees bent, hip distance apart, soles of the feet on the floor, and knees in line with the ankles.
2. Arms at your sides, palms down, draw your shoulder blades toward each other.
3. Engage your deep abs (Ab Draw), hamstrings, and glutes as you lift your hips toward the ceiling, lifting until your spine is neutral. Drive your heels into the floor and hold for 20 seconds to 1 minute.
4. Gently release your hips down to the floor and pull your knees into your chest to release the muscles in your low back.
5. After mastering this exercise with good form for at least 30 seconds, move on to the Alternating Single-Leg Bridge, on the next page.

Alternating Single-Leg Bridge

1. From the top of the Bridge position, extend your right leg toward the ceiling, ankle directly over your hip.
2. Bend your right knee as you lower your right leg, placing the sole of your foot on the floor.
3. Repeat with your left leg.
4. Alternate sides for a count of about 20.

Airplane

1. Kneeling on the floor, hands stacked directly beneath your shoulders and knees directly beneath your hips, push your hips back so your back arches slightly—without over-extending—engaging your low back muscles.
2. Retract your shoulder blades toward one another to engage the upper back muscles.
3. Draw your navel toward your spine (Ab Draw) to engage the ab muscles.
4. Extend your left leg back, parallel to the floor, checking to ensure hips are level.
5. Extend your right arm to the side, perpendicular to your body and parallel

to the floor. Check to ensure shoulders are level.

6. Hold for 20 to 40 seconds, then repeat on the opposite side.

Conclusion

Strengthening the core is an important part of training both for improved performance and injury prevention. Whether you are a coach implementing this program on the field or an athlete training at home, always remember quality over quantity. Athletes will benefit more from doing 8 pushups from their knees with full range of motion than doing 15 poorly positioned pushups from their toes.

> A well-trained core is the foundation for balance, strength, speed, agility, power, and almost every other athletic component to sport.

Following a safe progression will get you functionally strong faster, with less risk for injury. A well-trained core is the foundation for balance, strength, speed, agility, power, and almost every other athletic component to sport.

All the exercises in this book should be mastered before moving onto more advanced strength training—such as weighted squats, single-leg squats, and power cleans, or high impact jumping—such as single leg hops, depth jumps, and weighted jumps.

By building functional core strength, anyone can become a better athlete while decreasing the risk for injury.

Workouts For Home or Practice Field

Dynamic Warm-Up and Core Routine Soccer

Recommended at the beginning of every practice and before every game.

For video demonstrations of these exercises and a printable PDF of this workout go to OrganicFitnessMama.com.
*Use code: **8257660***

Dynamic Warm-Up and Core Routine

Start with the following four dynamic movements to warm up your legs and improve
functional flexibility.

- **Alternating Butt Kick**: 10x
- **Alternating High Knee With Hip Stretch**: 10x
- **Pendulum Kick**: 10x each leg
- **Side Pendulum Kick:** 10x each leg

Dynamic Warm-Up and Core Routine cont'd on next page

Grab a soccer ball and have a partner nearby for the next six movements to warm up and strengthen your core along with the rest of your body.

- **Standing Ab Draw**
- **Torso Rotation**: 20x
- **Wood Chopper**: 10x each—center, right, left
- **Partner Core Bracing**: 3 sets of 5 seconds each way each player—right, left, top, bottom
- **Single-Leg Ab Draw**
- **Single-Leg Ball Toss/Kick**: 10x each athlete each leg

Put the soccer ball aside and increase the intensity of movement with these exercises to strengthen and warm up all your muscles.

- **Skaters**: 20x
- **Squat**: 20x
- **Walking Lunge**: 20x
- **Side Shuffle with Knee Up**: 10x each direction
- **Jogging Butt Kicks**: 20 to 30 yards each direction
- **Jog to Gradual Sprint:** 50 to 60 yards

Strength and Core Routine Soccer

Recommended two to three times per week at the end of practice. If three sessions a week are not completed at practice, athletes should be encouraged to do a third session at home.

For video demonstrations of these exercises and a printable PDF of this workout go to OrganicFitnessMama.com.
*Use code: **8257660***

Strength and Core Routine

Do the Leg Circuit with no rest between each exercise. After week 4, increase to 2 sets of the circuit with no rest between sets.

Leg Circuit
Squat: 20x
Alternating Front Lunge: 20x
Squat Jump: 10x

Strength and Core Routine cont'd on next page

> After you complete the leg circuit, lower your heart rate with a few standing butt kicks before moving on to the floor exercises below.

- **Ab Draw**: 30 seconds or until mastered
- **Ab Draw with Alternating Leg Up:** 20x
- **Partner Leg Push**: 10 to 15 seconds each leg; each partner
- **Front Iso–Ab**: 20 to 45 seconds
- **Side Iso–Ab**: 20 to 45 seconds each side
- **Airplane**: 20 to 40 seconds each side
- **Pushups**: 5 to 20x
- **Bridge**: 20 to 40 seconds
- **Alternating Single–Leg Bridge**: 10 to 20x

A Note on Agility and Conditioning

Soccer is a sport that requires speed, endurance, and speed-endurance—the ability to sprint repeatedly with little rest between each maximum effort. I'll get into soccer energy systems and specific ways to train these energy systems in a future book. For now, understand that too much endurance training, such as long-distance running, can have a negative impact on an athlete's speed. In other words, long-distance running can make athletes slower. Speed training, however, will not negatively impact endurance. This phenomenon has to do with each person's balance of fast-twitch muscle fibers (genetically plentiful in elite sprinters) and slow-twitch muscle fibers (abundantly native to long distance runners) and the ability of these muscle fibers to adapt with training. Evidence suggests that fast-twitch muscle fibers can gradually convert to slow-twitch fibers while slow-twitch fibers do not change to fast-twitch fibers.

The most efficient way to add additional agility and conditioning beyond what is outlined in the above workouts is with small-sided pick-up games and drills that mimic soccer's energy systems. Because soccer is a combination of sprint/jog/walk with intermittent bursts of quick lateral, forward, and backward movements, use practice drills that replicate that pattern. For efficiency and mental stimulation, avoid running drills without a ball unless it's a game like tag or another activity that requires spontaneous forward, backward, and lateral movement.

Don't miss a single thing!

Join my **e-mail community** to receive more sports and health related information at:

www.OrganicFitnessmama.com

Join my **Facebook Group** to discuss and share ideas about topics including functional core training, strength & conditioning, dynamic warm-up, coaching, sports psychology, parenting and more!

From Facebook, search groups → **Guide to Youth Sports: A discussion group for athletes, parents, and coaches**

References

Ace Physical Therapy and Sports Medicine Institute. 2010-2017. *Core Strength and Physical Therapy,* Retrieved from http://www.ace-pt.org/ace-physical-therapy-and-sports-medicire-institute-core-strength-and-physical-therapy/

American Academy of Pediatrics (AAP). 2016. *AAP Clinical Report: Young Children Risk Injury in Single-Sport Specialization.* Retrieved from https://www.aap.org/en-us/about-the-aap/aap-press-room/pages/AAP-Clinical-Report-Young-Children-Risk-Injury-in-Single-Sport-Specialization.aspx

The American Journal of Sports Medicine. 2010. "Effect of 2 soccer matches in a week on physical performance and injury rate." G. Dupont. M. Nedelec, A. McCall, D. McCormack, S. Berthoin, U. Wisløff. Retrieved from https://www.ncbi.nlm.nih.gov/pubmed/20400751

American Medical Society for Sports Medicine. 2013. "Effectiveness of early sport specialization limited in most sports, sport diversification may be better approach at young ages." *ScienceDaily.* Retrieved from https://www.sciencedaily.com/releases/2013/04/130423172601.htm

Boyle, Michael. 2016. *New Functional Training for Sports-2nd Edition* (Kindle Locations 1483-1500) Human Kinetics. Kindle Edition.

Brumitt, Jason. 2017. *Core Assessment and Training.* Champagne, IL: Human Kinetics.

Encyclopedia Britannica. 2007. Diaphragm Anatomy. Retrieved from https:// www.britannica.com/science/diaphragm-anatomy.

FOOTBLOGBALL. 2013. "Interview with Tom Turner – USA National Soccer Instructor." Retrieved from https://footblogball.wordpress.com/2013/09/23/interview-with-tom-turner-usa-national-soccer-instructor/

Griesemer, Leanne. 2017. "The Importance of Core Strength," Apex Physical Therapy Concepts in Rehab, Retrieved from http://apexptflorida.com/the-importance-of-core-strength/

Heidloff, David. 2012. "The Off-Season: The Benefits of Taking Time Off." Athletico Physical Therapy. Retrieved from http://www.athletico.com/2012/01/11/the-off-season-the-benefits-of-taking-time-off/

Jayanthi, Neeru. 2013. "To protect against injuries, young athletes may need to play more just for fun", Public Release, Loyola University Health System. Retrieved from https://medicalxpress.com/news/2013-01-injuries-young-athletes-fun.html

Journal of Sports Sciences, 30:4, 379-386, DOI: 10.1080/02640414.2011.642808. 2012. "Differences in physical fitness and gross motor coordination in boys aged 6 to 12 years specializing in one versus sampling more than one sport." J. Fransen, J. Pion, J Vandendriessche, B. Vandrope, R. Vaeyens, M. Lenoir, RM Philippaerts. Retrieved from https://www.ncbi.nlm.nih.gov/pubmed/22214429

Journal of Strength & Conditioning Research (2):373-80. 2012. "Effect of Core Strength on the Measure of Power in the Extremities." J. Shinkle, TW Nesser, TJ Demchak , DM McMannus. Retrieved from https://www.ncbi.nlm.nih.gov/pubmed/22228111

Karpinksi, S. January, 11th 2018. Facebook Interview.

National Strength and Conditioning Association (NSCA). 2014. *Developing the Core*. Champagne, IL: Human Kinetics.

—— 2018. *Long-Term Athletic Development Position Statement*. Retrieved from https://www.nsca.com/long-term_athletic_development_position_statement/

O'Sullivan, John. 2014. *The Incredibly Massive Importance of Play, Changing the Game Project*. Morgan James Publishing. Retrieved from http://changingthegameproject.com/the-massive-importance-of-play/.

Physical Education and Sport Pedagogy, v12 n1 p77–87. 2007. M. Wall; J. Cote. "Developmental Activities that Lead to Dropout and Investment in Sport." Retrieved from https://eric.ed.gov/?id=EJ816014

Public Library of Science. 2017. "Individual Ball Possession in Soccer." D. Link; M. Hoernig. Retrieved from https://doi.org/10.1371/journal.pone.0179953

Salgado, Joey. 2016. *Intra-abdominal Pressure (IAP) Using Diaphragmatic Breathing*. Retrieved from https://www.youtube.com/watch?v=FB7apUiilWI&t=1s

Santas, D. 2015. *Breathe better to move better: breathe like a pro athlete*. CNN Health. Retrieved from http://www.cnn.com/2015/10/08/health/breathe-like-pro-athlete/index.html.

Ulm, Richard. 2013. *Dynamic Stability. Applying the Principles of dynamic neuromuscular Stabilization (DNS) to Strength & Conditioning*. {powerpoint slides}. Retrieved from https://www.nsca.com/uploadedFiles/NSCA/Inactive_Content/Program_Books/Saturday%2010%20Ulm.pdf.

University of Wisconsin School of Medicine and Public Health. 2017 "A Prospective Study on the Effect of Sport Specialization on Lower Extremity Injury Rates in High School Athletes." *The American Journal of Sports Medicine.* Retrieved from http://journals.sagepub.com/doi/abs/10.1177/0363546517710213?journalCode=ajsb

US Soccer Federation. 2006. *Best Practices for Coaching Soccer in the United States.*

US Youth Soccer. 2018. *Are Kids Specializing in Sports Too Early?* Retrieved from https://www.usyouthsoccer.org/are_kids_specializing_in_sports_too_early/
———2013. *Player Development Model*

Washmuth, Dan. 2017. *Multifidus: origin, insertion & action. S*tudy.com. Retrieved from https://study.com/academy/lesson/multifidus-muscle-origin-insertion-action.html.

Willardson, J.M.. 2007. "Core Stability Training: applications to sports conditioning programs." *Journal of Strength & Conditioning Research,* 21 (3): 979-85. Retrieved from https://www.ncbi.nlm.nih.gov/pubmed/17685697

Woitalla, Mike. 2013. "The Perils of Tournament Play: How to Cope. *Youth Soccer Insider.* Retrieved from https://www.socceramerica.com/publications/article/51792/the-perils-of-tournament-play-how-to-cope.html

Made in the USA
Lexington, KY
15 April 2018